Low Carb Diet 2.0 Recipes

A Low Carb Diet Book With 30 Low Carb Diet Recipes For Every Meal

Susan Brown

Table of Contents

Introduction 3

Chapter 1: An Overview of the Low Carb Diet 2.0 4

Chapter 2: The Low Carb Diet 2.0 Formula 6

Chapter 3: Low Carb Diet 2.0 Recipes 7

30 Delicious Low Carb 2.0 Diet Recipes 7

Conclusion 27

HIGHLY RECOMMENDED DIET BOOKS 28

Introduction

If you have been struggling with obesity, weight problems, type 2 diabetes, or other health problems, then this book is for you. This book will help you lose weight by implement strategies based around limiting your carb intake.

If you have been spending time on the internet or watching TV every now and then, you have probably heard of the low carb diets across the globe. It is very popular in countries like the United States, Australia, China, Korea, United Kingdom, Philippines, Spain, Slovenia, Italy, and most especially in Sweden. Ordinary people and celebrities from different countries who want to get fit and stay fit have tried low carb nutritional diets. In fact, food companies who are selling healthy foods are creating diet programs that are based on the low carb nutritional approach. In fact, reality television shows that focus on weight loss have featured the low carb diets to accelerate the weight loss process.

This book contains a brief history of low carb nutritional diets. You will also get to learn about its advantages and some concerns raised by its critics. This book also contains very practical tips on what you need to do before you start adopting this nutritional approach. Plus, this book has 30 delicious recipes that are easy to prepare. These recipes are so good that you would not even feel that you are on a diet. You will be surprised that you can still eat a lot of your favorite food while on this diet. You can eat bacon, cheese, ham, yogurt, and eggs.

Enjoy this book and good luck on your journey to become a fitter and healthier you!

Chapter 1: An Overview of the Low Carb 2.0 Diet

Every year since 2003, low-carb diets continue to increase in popularity. Many celebrities like Kim Kardashian, Shakira, Sharon Osborne, Renee Zellweger, Courtney Thorne- Smith, and Oprah are big fans of the low-carb diets. Studies show that low-carb diets are very effective for weight loss and in managing the symptoms of diseases such as diabetes.

Low-carb diets are focused on controlling the dieter's carbohydrate consumption. It is believed that the body's metabolism can be altered by limiting the consumption of complex carbohydrates. When you consume less carbohydrates, the body converts stored body fat to energy. This process is called ketosis.

Most of the people who wanted to lose weight go into diet fads, lose weight, and then gain it back after. Low carb diets are designed to help dieters maintain their weight to make sure that the dieters will not gain back the weight that they worked so hard to lose. It is also used to manage the symptoms of disease such as diabetes. Therefore it has been known to reduce the insulin and blood sugar levels.

In addition low carb diets are also known to control a person's blood pressure and it is an effective treatment for metabolic disorders.

Low carb diets are popular because they are an effective tool that one can use for weight loss. A lot of people have transformed themselves simply by limiting their carb intake.

Here are some of the disadvantages claimed by some nutritionists:

1. You can't eat high saturated fat consumption.

2. It is restrictive.

3. During the first few weeks, you may feel naucious.

4. It is not for vegetarians.

However, the advantages of low carb diets far outweigh the disadvantages. Listed below are the benefits and advantages:

1. You'll lose weight rapidly

2. It is not time consuming

3. The foods that are allowed in this diet are not expensive

4. You can eat protein rich and fatty foods

5. It is known to manage Type 2 Diabetes

These recipes in this book are designed to get you on your way to lasting health and vitality. When you achieve your ideal body through the low carb diet, you will gain more self confidence. You will smile more, go out more, and mingle with other people more often. Most importantly, you will be able to live a more healthy and fulfilling life.

Chapter 2: The Low Carb Diet 2.0 Formula

Whether you are adopting this diet for vanity or for important health reasons, it is essential to follow the step outlined below before starting with the Low Carb Diet:

1. Set Your Goals – You have to find out what your ideal weight and body mass index is and you have to aim for that. It is important to know what your weight goals are. Your weight loss goal will keep you motivated. As you know, avoiding unhealthy, but extremely tasty foods like donuts, white pasta, and cakes is difficult. You have to be focused on your goal to avoid all types of food temptations.

2. Search for Recipes – It is not recommended to eat the same thing every day. If you are on a diet, it doesn't mean that you cannot eat delicious food. This book contains recipes that you can use while you are on the diet.

3. Count Your Carbohydrates – It is also helpful to count your carbohydrate intake. You could download a carbohydrate counter application from https://cronometer.com/.

4. Get Support – It is important to join a support group. You could actually meet people online that are on low carb diets. There are also a lot of clubs that promote the Low Carb nutritional diets. You could join these clubs as well. Lastly, ask for the support of your loved ones and the people you interact with on a daily basis. It is also great if you can later on encourage your co-workers to join you in your weight loss journey.

5. Exercise – For optimum results, it is always best to exercise. Exercise will not only help you in attaining your weight loss goal, but it would also increase your energy, elevate your mood, and ensure that you will get maximum benefits from the low carb diet.

Chapter 3: Low Carb Diet 2.0 Recipes

If you are on a diet, it does not mean that you have to eat bland foods. Low Carb Diet 2.0 nutritional diet is awesome because you can eat many of your favorite foods. This diet strictly prohibits certain kind of carbohydrates like white bread, white rice, and pasta. However, you can consume foods that are rich in protein like meat and dairy products. Here are the low carbohydrate recipes that you can use while on this low carb diet.

30 Delicious Low Carb Diet 2.0 Recipes

Cod and Broccoli

This dish is tasty and rich in fiber and protein. You can eat this during lunch or dinner. To make this dish, you'll need:

6 ounces of skinned cod fillet

2 tablespoons of Herb Butter Blend

2 cups of broccoli florets

Preheat the oven at 350 degrees Fahrenheit. Arrange the broccoli on a large piece of aluminum foil and top it with the cod fillet and herb butter blend. Season the dish with salt and pepper. Fold the foil and carefully seal the packet. Bake this for 10 minutes until the fish and the broccoli are tender. Serve and enjoy. This dish serves one person so feel free to adjust the amount of ingredients if you are cooking for two people or more.

Deviled Eggs

This dish is perfect for breakfast. To make this recipe, you'll need the following ingredients:

4 teaspoons of finely chopped capers

6 hard-boiled eggs

1 finely chopped green onion

2 tablespoons of finely chopped celery

3 tablespoons mayonnaise

2 ounces of finely chopped ham

1 teaspoon Dijon mustard

You need to cut the hard boiled eggs and scoop out the yolks so you would have 12 "egg bowls". Mix the onion, celery, ham, mustard, egg yolk, and mayonnaise and season with pepper and salt. Put the egg yolk mixture into the egg white bowls. This dish is good for four people. This dish is also great to pack and bring to your office for lunch or quick snack.

Chocolate Mudslide

This drink can be a great midday snack. To make this refreshing drink, you'll need:

One half cup of water

One cup of heavy cream

Three tablespoons cocoa powder

One half cup of chocolate syrup (sugar-free)

One teaspoon of vanilla extract

Mix the water, cream, cocoa powder, and chocolate syrup in a medium saucepan. Stir the mixture until the cocoa powder has dissolved. Remove the pan from the heat and add the vanilla extracts and chocolate. Pour the mixture in a pan and freeze for three hours. Once it is frozen, place the mixture in a blender until it is softened and slush. Pour into glasses and serve. This recipe makes four glasses of great chocolate drink.

Macho Chili

Chili is a great Mexican recipe that everyone enjoys. This dish is low in carbohydrates. This is recipe can serve 10 people so you can serve this dish during a small dinner party. To make this dish, you'll need the following ingredients:

Two teaspoons of kosher salt

5 pounds of beef cut in cubes

Three tablespoons of virgin olive oil

One half teaspoon of ground black pepper

1 chopped yellow onion

1 can of diced tomatoes

Three tablespoon chili powder

½ cup chicken broth

Four minced roasted garlic cloves

Heat the oven at 325 degrees Fahrenheit. Season the beef with salt and pepper. Heat 1 and ½ tablespoons of olive oil in a pan and add the beef. Make sure that all sides of the meat are brown. In a separate pan, heat the remaining olive oil and add the chili powder, chicken broth, tomatoes, and garlic. Add the beef. Put the beef mixture in a baking pan and bake for 2 and a half hours. It is best to put cheese on top of this dish before serving.

Baked Salmon Puree

This dish is great to serve during lunch. This recipe is rich in protein and it serves four people. In order to make this dish, be sure to prepare the following ingredients:

1 tablespoon butter, unsalted

Two tablespoons virgin olive oil

4 portions of Salmon fillet

1 and ½ pounds of bok choy, cut into 2 pieces

¼ teaspoon salt

2 ounces of roasted red pepper

¼ teaspoon ground black pepper

2 ounces salsa

½ teaspoon lemon zest

Heat the oven at 475 degrees Fahrenheit. Put the virgin olive oil and unsalted butter in a pan. Place the pan in the oven until the butter melts. Season the fish fillet with salt and pepper and place it in a pan with the melted butter. Bake the fish for ten minutes and make sure to cook each side. Add the lemon zest and chopped bok choy and bake for 1 minute. Set this aside. In the meantime, place the salsa and puree pepper in a blender until it is carefully mixed. Place the fish and the green on a plate and put a dollop of the puree mixture over each fish. Serve and enjoy.

Breakfast Frittata

This is a healthy egg recipe that you can prepare in only 15 minutes. You can do this in the morning before going to work. It is easy and quick to prepare. To make this great breakfast frittata, you'll need:

½ cup of diced red pepper

8 large eggs

½ cup of diced green pepper

1 cup of grated cheddar cheese

1 cup of cubed cooked ham

Salt and pepper, as needed

Butter, as needed

Beat all 8 eggs with a whisk, then stir in the rest of the ingredients. Melt the butter in a skillet and add the egg mixture. Cook for five to ten minutes. Slide the breakfast frittata on a plate. This recipe makes 4 servings. This delicious dish will make you feel good and full. Serving this delicious fritata is a great way to start your day.

Spinach Egg Casserole

This is one of the best egg casserole recipes and this is really easy to do. You can serve this either during lunch, breakfast, or dinner. To make this incredibly delicious casserole, you'll need:

2 large eggs

20 ounces of leaf spinach

1/3 cup of grated Parmesan cheese

Salt and pepper, as needed

1 teaspoon of crushed garlic

1/3 cup of non fat milk

Preheat the oven at 350 degrees Fahrenheit. In a huge bowl, whisk the egg, cheese, milk, garlic, pepper, and salt. Fold in the spinach and put the mixture in four casserole dishes. Remember to spray olive oil or vegetable oil on the casserole dishes before pouring the mixture. Bake the mixture for twenty minutes until it is lightly set. This recipe makes 4 servings. It is best to enjoy this dish with your family or friends.

Egg White Scramble

This egg white scramble dish is one of the perfect ways to start your mornings. This dish is healthy and easy to make. This dish has a lot of proteins and nutrients. To make this dish this, you'll need:

1 red pepper

1 carton egg whites

1 head broccoli

1 onion

Salt, as needed

10 Asparagus spears

1 teaspoon of olive oil

Vegetable and Chicken Frittata

This recipe is full of protein and nutrients. This is great to start you work day right. You can strictly follow this recipe or you can add other vegetables that are available in your refrigerator. To make this dish, you need to prepare the following:

One cup broccoli florets

2 finely chopped green onions

¾ cups sliced fresh mushrooms

1 tablespoon butter

16 egg whites

1 cup cooked lean chicken

¼ cup water

½ teaspoon garlic salt

½ teaspoon Italian seasoning

1 and ½ cups low fat shredded Cheddar cheese

½ cup chopped tomatoes

Heat the mushrooms, broccoli, and onions in the butter until the broccoli is tender. Add the chicken. Remove the skillet from heat. In a separate bowl, combine eggs, mustard, water, Italian seasoning and garlic salt. Add the cheese, broccoli mixture, and tomatoes. Pour the mixture into a greased baking dish. Bake this at 375 degrees Fahrenheit for twenty seven minutes. This dish makes four servings.

Cottage Cheese Chicken Salad

This is a healthy and tasty dish that is easy and convenient to make. To make this dish you'll need:

1 cup of cooked and chopped chicken breast

2 chopped hard boiled eggs

1 cup low fat cottage cheese

½ cup low fat mayonnaise

¼ cup diced celery

One half cup low fat cheddar cheese

Combine the chicken, celery, mayonnaise, and eggs in a bowl. Add the cheddar cheese, cottage cheese, and salt. Carefully mix the ingredients, serve, and enjoy!

Crunchy Parmesan Chicken

This dish is great for dinner. You can also eat this with salad or pasta. This dish is great for date night or special occasions. It only takes 20 minutes to prepare this recipe. To make this dish, you'll need:

4 trimmed and pounded chicken breasts

2 cups of grated Parmesan cheese

3 eggs whites

Preheat the oven to 400 degrees Fahrenheit. Coat the chicken with egg whites. Arrange the coated chicken on a baking pan. Bake the chicken for 20 minutes. You can serve this dish with your pasta or favorite salad.

Peachy Grilled Chicken

This dish is tasty and full of flavor. This is a delicious low carbohydrate dish that you and your friends can enjoy. To make this dish, you'll need the following ingredients:

2 and ½ teaspoons grated fresh ginger

3 tablespoons of sherry vinegar

2 teaspoons of finely chopped fresh rosemary

½ teaspoons of crushed red pepper

½ teaspoon salt

2 teaspoons of granular sugar substitute

½ cup of olive oil

Freshly ground black pepper

Four lean chicken breast halves

2 ripe peaches, chopped

2 cups of French feta cheese

1 medium head romaine lettuce

To make the dressing, combine the ginger, vinegar, rosemary, sugar substitute, salt, and pepper flakes in a small bowl. Whisk in the oil until the dressing thickens. Brush one tablespoon of dressing on the chicken and set aside for one hour. After an hour, heat the grill. Season the chicken with salt and pepper. Grill the chicken for 15 minutes. Remove the chicken from the grill and place it on a platter to rest. Place the peaches on the grill until it is softened. Toss the greens with the remaining dressing and divide the salad on four plates. Top each salad with a chicken slice and a peach slice. Sprinkle the salad with cheese. Serve and Enjoy!

Garlic and Lemon Rosemary Chicken

This is a simple and delicious dish that is best for dinner. To make this recipe, you'll need:

½ cup of chicken broth

One pound chicken

One lemon

1 tablespoon garlic

2 rosemary sprigs

2 teaspoons of lemon pepper

Salt, as needed

Ground black pepper, as needed

Coat the chicken with lemon juice, garlic, lemon pepper, and rosemary. Place the chicken in a baking pan and pour the chicken broth into the pan. Bake the chicken for 25 minutes. Serve and enjoy this dish!

Pulled Chicken

This is a great recipe that is healthy and delicious. This is also one of the allergy free chicken recipes. To make this dish, you'll need:

¼ cup of natural ketchup

4 chicken breasts

¼ cup of cider vinegar

3 tablespoons of olive oil

¼ cup of brown sugar

½ chopped onion

1 teaspoon of cinnamon

1 teaspoon of chili powder

1 teaspoon of smoked paprika

1 teaspoon of salt

1 teaspoon of cumin

Put the chicken breasts in a slow cooker. Add the cider vinegar, ketchup, brown sugar, chopped onion, and olive oil. Season the chicken with chili powder, smoked paprika, cinnamon, cumin, and salt. Cook this for 4 to 5 hours. When cooked, shred the chicken breast and serve in a bowl.

Mongolian Chicken

This dish is a healthier alternative to your takeout Chinese. This is a healthy and delicious dish that you can serve during date night. To make this dish, you'll need:

¼ cup of quinoa flour

16 ounces of chicken

½ teaspoon of ginger

½ cup of soy sauce

1 tablespoon of crushed garlic

1 tablespoon of red pepper flakes

½ cup of water

½ cup of green onion

Dissolve the brown sugar in water. Add the low sodium soy sauce, then add the red pepper flakes. Slice the chicken into bite size and toss on the quinoa flour. Spray the olive oil in a skillet and heat. Add the garlic and the ginger. Add the chicken and the soy sauce mixture. Cook until the chicken is tender. Transfer onto a plate and serve.

Broccoli Cheddar Dip

This is great for a party. This dish is full of flavor and it is gluten free. To make this dish, you'll need the following ingredients:

8 ounces of grated cheddar

10 ounces of frozen broccoli

2 tablespoons of milk

4 ounces of cream cheese

½ tablespoon of ground black pepper

½ teaspoon of hot sauce

Place the frozen broccoli in a microwave-safe container. Cover it with plastic wrap and heat in a microwave for about 9 minutes until tender. Uncover the container and ass the cream cheese, cheddar cheese, hot sauce, and milk. Cover the container again and microwave for 1 to 2 minutes until the cheeses are melted. Stir the mixture until smooth and thick. Serve this dish with crackers or fresh vegetable salad.

This dish only has 72 calories. It only has 1 gram of carbohydrates and it is rich in protein and calcium.

Antipasto Skewers

This dish is great for lunch and is good for 8 persons so you can prepare this for your family and friends. To prepare this dish, you'll need:

1 teaspoon of salt

1 teaspoon of ground pepper

1 teaspoon of dried oregano

1 clove of garlic

1 tablespoon of lemon juice

1 tablespoon of balsamic vinegar

1 tablespoon of olive oil

8 mushrooms

4 servings of salami genoa

100 grams of cougrette

8 kalamata olives

8 cherry tomatoes

1 bell pepper

8 proscuitto slice

Soak the bamboo skewers in water for about fifteen minutes. Thread each skewer with proscuitto, one olive, one courgette, one tomato, one salami cube, one mushroom, and one cherry tomato. Place the skewers in a dish. In a separate bowl, lemon juice, oil, vinegar, oregano, garlic, pepper, and salt. Pour this mixture over the skewers. Make sure to coat each skewer with the lemon juice mixture. Grill the skewers until the vegetables are tender. Serve and enjoy.

Asian Tuna Salad

This is a great low carbohydrate dish is high in protein and good fats. To prepare this dish, you'll need:

1 tomato

1 tablespoon of soy sauce

6 radishes

3 bok choy

30 grams of tinned water chestnuts

175 gram of tuna fillet

Steam the bok choy and grill the tuna. Fry this and the other ingredients. Serve and enjoy. This recipe is only good for one person. Feel free to double the amount of ingredients if you are planning to serve this to two people.

Asian Turkey Burgers

This is a healthier alternative to the usual fast food burgers. To make this dish, you'll need:

3 romaine leaves

1 teaspoon of ground black pepper

1 clove of garlic

3 tablespoons of soy sauce

1 green bell pepper

1 tablespoon of fresh ginger root

2 tablespoons of fresh parsley

300 grams of ground turkey

1 onion

Chop the green pepper, garlic, and onion finely. Combine all ingredients in a bowl and form the mixture 3 burger patties. Grill the patties until cooked and serve the patties on large romaine leaves.

Asparagus Soup

This is a great dish to eat during the winter season. To make this dish, you'll need:

One tablespoon of olive oil

2 fresh onions

150 milligram of single cream

1000 milligram of vegetable broth

1 teaspoon of salt

8 celery stalks

2 teaspoons of fresh tarragon

40 asparagus

1 teaspoon ground pepper

Heat the oil in a pan. Add the onion, broth, salt, asparagus, pepper, half of the tarragon, and celery. Boil the mixture and let it simmer until the asparagus is tender. Add the remaining tarragon and cream. Serve and enjoy.

Egg and Bacon Casserole

This tasty meal is great for breakfast. To make this dish, you'll need:

One teaspoon of black pepper

One teaspoon of dried thyme

One teaspoon of salt

Six bacons

8 tablespoons of ground flaxseed

200 grams of cheddar cheese

5 mushrooms

Half green bell pepper

Half onion

7 eggs

170 milligrams of unsweetened soya milk

Heat the oven at 350 degrees Fahrenheit. Heat the peppers, onion, mushrooms, and peppers in a pan with a little oil and layer all the vegetables, cooked bacon, and cheese. Blend the milk, spices, almond, and eggs and pour the mixture over the top. Bake this for thirty minutes and keep it warm for about five to ten minutes. Serve and enjoy!

Tomato, Bacon, and Cheddar Stacks

This recipe is great for breakfast. This recipe serves six people so you can share this with your friends and family. To make this dish, you'll need the following ingredients:

3 tomatoes

Six bacons

90 grams of cheddar cheese

Cook the bacon in a frying pan until it is brown. Add the cheddar and tomato and steam until the cheese is melted. It only takes 5 minutes to prepare this. It is that quick and easy.

Broccoli Soup

This dish is great for lunch. To make this dish, you'll need:

1 teaspoon of fresh parsley

2 tablespoons of Parmesan cheese

1 teaspoon of salt

1 teaspoon of black pepper

200 grams of diced tomatoes

800 milligrams of low sodium chicken stock

200 grams of ham

4 cloves of garlic

1 tablespoon of olive oil

Heat the olive oil and add the ham. Add the garlic, chicken stock, broccoli, and tomatoes and bring to boil. Cook for ten minutes, sprinkle with Parmesan & parsley, and serve.

Chicken Burgers

This is a great dish to serve during lunch. To make this dish, you'll need the following ingredients:

2 avocados

2 cucumbers

400 grams of ground chicken

400 grams of mixed salad leaves

200 grams of sun dried tomatoes

8 romaine leaves

2 tablespoons of olive oil

2 cloves of garlic

20 cherry tomatoes

8 spring onions

2 chilli peppers

2 teaspoons of mixed herbs

1 tablespoons of lemon zest

1 teaspoons of ground coriander

Combine the garlic, onion, mixed herbs, sundried tomatoes, and ground chicken in a bow. Form the mixture into four burgers. On a separate bowl, mix the lemon zest, cherry tomatoes, coriander, and chili pepper in a large bowl. Carefully brush the burgers with olive oil. Grill the burgers for 3 minutes each side. Serve each burger with a romaine leaf. Serve with mixed chopped salad, cucumber, avocado, and tomato salsa.

Almond and Cottage Cheese

To make this dish, you'll need these ingredients:

8 tablespoons of almond butter

160 grams of blueberries

460 grams of cottage cheese

It is really easy to make this dish. All you need to do is combine the cottage cheese and the almond butter and then top the mixture with the blueberries. Serve and enjoy!

Spinach and Chickpeas Salad

This recipe can be prepared in only five minutes. To make this dish, you'll need:

1 romaine lettuce

200 grams of baby spinach

100 grams of tinned chickpeas

8 cherry tomatoes

1 red bell pepper

1 tablespoon of virgin oil

All you need to do is combine all the ingredients. This recipe can serve two people.

Fried Asparagus and Scallops

To make this dish, you'll need the following:

16 stalks of asparagus

One red bell pepper

12 scallions

2 cloves of garlic

12 raw scallops

2 tablespoons of olive oil

2 tablespoons of soy sauce

One green bell pepper

10 plain peanuts

Slice each asparagus stalk into half. Heat the olive oil in the skillet. Add the scallops, sliced bell peppers, scallops, garlic, and scallions. Fry until the asparagus is tender. Add the peanuts and soy sauce. Serve and enjoy!

Blueberry Yogurt

It only takes five minutes to prepare this dish. To make this dish, you'll need:

130 grams of Greek yogurt

39 grams of blueberries

Simply add the blueberries to the yogurt. This dish is great for evening snack.

Celery with Peanut Butter

It only takes 5 minutes to prepare this dish. To prepare this dish, you'll need:

2 tablespoons of peanut butter

2 celery stalks

This is easy to prepare. Just fill the celery stalks with peanut butter, serve, and enjoy!

Lettuce Wrapped Tacos

This dish is a perfect substitute to your favorite Mexican dish. You'll need the following ingredients:

2 tomatoes

1 cucumber

2 yellow onions

2 romaine lettuce

4 avocados

60 grams of cheddar cheese

2 chili peppers

10 tablespoons of sour cream

4 teaspoons of chili powder

200 grams of ground beef

2 yellow bell peppers

Two red bell peppers

Cook the meat in a skillet together with the onion, sliced peppers, and half of the jalapeno. Add the cumin and chili powder. Add the avocado, tomato, sour cream, cheese, and the chopped cucumber. Use the lettuce as a substitute forr tacos. Arrange, serve, and enjoy!

Olives with Grapes and Cheese

This is very easy to make. You'll need the following ingredients:

7 black olives

10 seedless grapes

30 grams of gouda cheese

Just combine all the ingredients and enjoy!

Conclusion

The Low Carb Diet 2.0 nutritional diet is a great diet plan that will help you lose weight without having to go through starvation or long hours at the gym. This diet is popular not only because it is effective, but also because it is easy to follow. Other diet plans would recommend more expensive organic foods.

The low carbohydrate recipes that are contained in this book are also very delicious and easy to make. You do not have to give up some of the most delicious foods like bacon, ham, and cheese.

The low carb diets have helped many celebrities, young professionals, middle-aged parents, and eager students achieve their ideal body and health.

A lot of women who have gained weight due to pregnancy went back to their old body size with the aid of the low carb diets. A lot of people who are suffering from type 2 diabetes have successfully controlled their blood sugar levels by reducing their carb intake.

These recipes will help you become the best version of yourself. They will transform your life by making you a happier, healthier person.

You are now taking the first step to attain the body and lifestyle that you have always wanted.

HIGHLY RECOMMENDED DIET BOOKS

RECCOMMENDED LOW CARB DIET 2.0 BOOKS:

Low Carb Diet 2.0: A 14-Day Low Carb Diet Plan For A Simple Start (A Guide To The Low Carb Diet 2.0 Plus A Diet Plan To Achieve Your Weight Loss Goals)

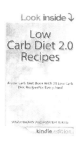

Low Carb Diet 2.0 Recipes: A Low Carb Diet Book With 30 Low Carb Diet Recipes For Every Meal

Low Carb Diet 2.0 Recipes: A 7-Day Low Carb Diet Plan For a Sexy Body! (50 Low Carb Recipes Included)

RECOMMENDED PALEO DIET BOOKS:

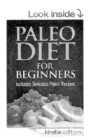

Paleo Diet For Beginners: Includes Delicious Paleo Recipes

Paleo Diet For Beginners: Eat Well and Feel Great With The Ultimate 7-Day Paleo Diet Plan

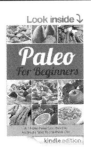

Paleo For Beginners: A 14-Day Paleo Diet Plan For A Simple Start To The Paleo Diet

Gluten Free Cookbook: A Simple Guide To Gluten Free Breads, Pasta, Baking, and More! (Includes Over 75 Gluten Free Recipes)

RECOMMENDED DASH DIET BOOKS:

DASH Diet For Beginners: A 14-Day Dash Diet Plan For A Simple Start To The Dash Diet

Dash Diet: The Dash Diet Simple Solution To Weight Loss - Includes Over 50 Dash Diet Recipes To Maximize The Weight Loss Process

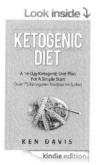

Ketogenic Diet: A 14-Day Ketogenic Diet Plan For A Simple Start

RECOMMENDED DUKAN DIET BOOKS:

The Dukan Diet: A 21-Day Dukan Diet Plan & 100+ Dukan Diet Recipes To Get Started Immediately

The Dukan Diet Made Simple: The Dukan Diet Attack Phase (Includes A 7-Day Meal Plan)

RECOMMENDED ALKALINE FOOD AND DIET BOOKS:

Alkaline Foods For The Alkaline Diet: Feel The pH Miracle of a Healthy pH Diet

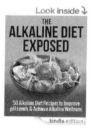

The Alkaline Diet Exposed: 50 Alkaline Diet Recipes to Improve pH Levels and Achieve Alkaline Wellness

RECOMMENDED ZONE DIET BOOKS:

Zone Diet: One 75 Zone Diet Recipes Included & A 14-Day Zone Diet Meal Plan To Lose Weight And Prevent Disease

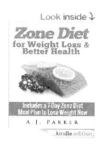

Zone Diet: For Weight Loss & Better Health (Includes a 7-Day Meal Plan to Lose Weight Now)

Zone Diet Cookbook - Includes 50 Zone Diet Recipes For Every Meal

RECOMMENDED BLOOD TYPE DIET BOOKS:

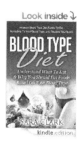

Blood Type Diet: Understand What To Eat & Why You Should Eat Foods Based On Your Blood Type (Includes Blood Type Diet Foods To Eat According To Your Blood Type and Recipes You'll Love)

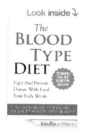

The Blood Type Diet: 23 Recipes For Each Blood Type - Fight And Prevent Disease With Food Your Body Wants

RECOMMENDED DIABETES DIET BOOKS:

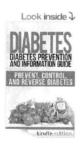

Diabetes: Diabetes Prevention and Information Guide: Prevent, Control, and Reverse Diabetes

The White Devil: A 30-Day Sugar Detox Made Simple (Quit Sugar or Quit Life!)

Diabetes Diet: A Diabetes Cookbook Filled With 30 Delicious Diabetes Diet Recipes

MORE SPECIALIZED DIETS:

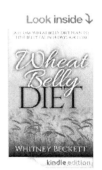

Wheat Belly Diet: A 14-Day Wheat Belly Diet Plan To Lose Belly Fat In 14 Days (Or Less)

Mediterranean Diet: A 14-Day Mediterranean Diet Meal Plan - Includes Over 50 Mediterranean Diet Recipes!

Anti-Inflammatory Diet: Includes Anti-Inflammatory Recipes

Macrobiotic Diet: Eat Healthy, Get Healthy, Improve Your Health - Includes Delicious Recipes

RECOMMENDED WEIGHT LOSS BOOKS:

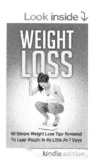

Weight Loss: 50 Simple Weight Loss Tips Revealed To Lose Weight In As Little As 7 Days

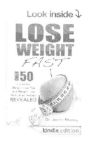

Lose Weight Fast: Over 50 Incredible Weight Loss Tips and Weight Loss Motivation Secrets Revealed

RECOMMENDED HOLISTIC HEALTH BOOKS:

Medicinal Herbs: Includes Aromatherapy, Essential Oils, And Herbal Medicines To Improve Your Health

Old Grandma's Medicinal Herbs: 59 Herbal Remedies With A Touch of Grandma's Magic

Reiki: A Reiki Guide To Access The Self-Healing Powers Of Reiki (Written For Reiki Beginners)

Organic Foods: Why Should I Eat Organic Foods? (The Pro's, the Con's, & Everything You'd Want To Know

How To Live In The Present Moment: Let Go Of The Past & Stop Worrying About The Future

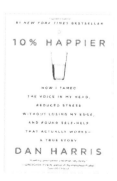

10% Happier: How I Tamed the Voice in My Head, Reduced Stress Without Losing My Edge, and Found Self-Help That Actually Works--A True Story

SPECIAL LIMITED TIME OFFERS

Blood Type Diet: Blood Type Diet: Understand What To Eat & Why You Should Eat Foods Based On Your Blood Type; & The Blood Type Diet Book: 23 Recipes For ...

Sugar Detox: The White Devil - A 30-Day Sugar Detox Made Simple (Quit Sugar or Quit Life!) & Diabetes Diet - A Diabetes Cookbook Filled With 30 Delicious ...

Paleo Diet For Beginners: Paleo Diet For Beginners: Eat Well & Feel Great With The Ultimate 7-Day Paleo Meal Plan, & Paleo Diet For Beginners: Includes ...

The Alkaline Diet: The Alkaline Diet Exposed: 50 Alkaline Diet Recipes to Improve pH Levels and Achieve Alkaline Wellness, & Alkaline Foods For The Alkaline ...

DASH Diet: The Dash Diet Simple Solution To Weight Loss Includes Over 50 Dash Diet Recipes To Maximize The Weight Loss Process, & DASH Diet For Beginners:

Zone Diet: Zone Diet Cookbook: Includes 50 Zone Diet Recipes For Every Meal, & Zone Diet for Weight Loss & Better Health: Includes a 7-Day Meal Plan to

Look inside ↓

kindle edition

<u>Anti-Inflammatory Diet: Includes Anti-Inflammatory Recipes, & Why Should I Eat Organic Foods - The Pro's, The Con's, & Everything You'd Want To Know</u>

23036565R00026

Printed in Great Britain
by Amazon